I0626078

IN HIS IMAGE

VOLUME I: MIGHTY LIKE HIM

An I-spy series filled with affirmations for all ages.

GOD
made me in
HIS
image,

2

So, I am **not** damaged,

4

I am not broken and bruised,

you are so brave

you are so brave

Lost or confused.

1 Corinthians 16:13

Psalm 27:14

Proverbs 3:5–6

Luke 9:23

Psalm 27:1

8

I am
secure,
I am
anchored,

9

10

I am
bold,
and I am
brave.

11

12

I am
fierce
and
unafraid.

13

14

His Spirit lives within me,

15

16

And His truth sets me free.

17

18

I may be small, but He is mighty.

19

20

I may be young, but He is for me.

21

22

My head is anointed, and my feet are ready,

23

24

Because He's the Rock that holds me steady.

25

Now that you've read your affirmations, it's time to have some fun!

26

Go back through the book to find these items:

Page 1: 1 set of keys, 4 gold buttons, 1 light post, the Statue of Liberty, 1 dove

Pages 2-3: 2 paper airplanes, 1 pair of scissors, 12 stars, 1 magnifying glass, 1 old clock

Pages 4-5: 1 bird cage, the Milky Way, 1 stamp, 1 cassette, 1 cannon

Pages 6-7: 1 compass, 3 question marks, 1 cross, 1 ship, 1 treasure chest

Pages 8-9: 1 church, 1 typewriter, 1 mirror, 1 bicycle, 1 rose

Pages 10-11: 2 chess pieces, 1 unicycle, 1 trumpet, 1 disco ball, 1 Bible

Pages 12-13: 1 chair, 1 moth, 2 stacks of books, 1 helmet (armor), 1 car

Pages 14-15: 1 oil lamp, 1 padlock, 2 sets of mountains, 1 needle and thread, 1 radio

Pages 16-17: 1 breastplate, 1 lion, 1 candle, 3 butterflies, 7 coins

Pages 18-19: 1 moped, 1 camera, 1 crown, 1 lightbulb, 1 hourglass

Pages 20-21: 2 planes, 1 pair of headphones, 1 chandelier, 3 computers, 2 pyramids

Pages 22-23: 1 pair of shoes, 1 bucket, 1 tea kettle, 4 keys, 1 desk

Pages 24-25: 1 piano, 1 old phone, 1 wagon wheel, 1 old TV, 1 camera film

This isn't just an I-spy book, but it's a poem filled with affirmations that you can also memorize. Sometimes we forget how valuable we truly are, and we forget that we are children of God. So, let this be a reminder that you are awesome, and more importantly, you are His and made in His image.

God made me in His image,
So, I am not damaged,
I am not broken and bruised,
Lost or confused.
I am secure, I am anchored,
I am bold, and I am brave.
I am fierce and unafraid.
His Spirit lives within me,
And His truth sets me free.
I may be small, but He is mighty.
I may be young, but He is for me.
My head is anointed, and my feet are ready,
Because He's the Rock that holds me steady.

29

www.thej19.com

The J19 is a ministry and organization that is founded upon the Bible verse Joshua 1:9, where God speaks directly to Joshua, reminding him of the promise to come and to be strong and courageous in that promise even in the face of impossibility.

We all have a calling on our life, and it's up to us whether we decide to embark on this journey with Him or not, and this organization exists to be an echo of Joshua 1:9, reminding every child, man, and woman that we can do those hard things. The J19 exists to be an encouragement to every person that even in the wildest of circumstances, God never forsakes us and never breaks a promise. He is fighting for us, cheering us on, and He so desperately wants us to carry a relationship with Him.

It doesn't matter where you've walked, what you've been through, or what you've done. We are here to point you *upward* so that you can move *forward* in what God has just for you.

Connect with us on:

30

ABOUT THE AUTHOR

Sam Rivers Jones is a believer, the founder of The J19, a content creator and blogger, a creative, a mom to two beautiful girls, and a wife. She presently serves at The Avenue with her husband, and when she isn't working on her socials or writing, she loves spending time with her family on their farm.

Stay connected with Sam at www.samriversjones.com and also on:

In His Image Volume I: Mighty Like Him
Copyright © 2024 by Sam Rivers Jones. All rights reserved. No portion of this book may be reproduced, stored in a retrieval system, or transmitted in any form or by any means, except for brief quotations in printed reviews, without prior permission of Sam Rivers Jones. Requests may be submitted by email: samriversjones@gmail.com.

All Scripture verses are taken from the New King James Version®. Copyright © 1982 by Thomas Nelson. Used by permission. All rights reserved.

Editing and formatting services by ChristianEditingandDesign.com.

www.ingramcontent.com/pod-product-compliance
Lightning Source LLC
Chambersburg PA
CBHW041500120626
46547CB00003B/487